The Faith Based

Relationship Trust Boundary Model

How to Guard Your Heart

Olivia Verbeck

CONTENTS

For Pastor Alex and Donna Lucero

A team who has the heart of good shepherds. You both have shown love, guidance, protection, and support to so many for so many years. Your sound teachings have been food for my soul and have cultivated a rich atmosphere where my children and I, along with so many others, have been able to take root and grow. Thank you both for your courage to speak the truth and for the loving kindness you have shown to so many. Your love for God's people is humbling and truly inspiring.

This book is dedicated to you both with love.

Thank you to Art and Elaine Villarruel for encouraging me to write this book.

Thank you to Mary Roberts and Gregg & Julie Laub for the years of bible study you all have led. I thank God for your faithfulness.

Special thank you to my girls Jacobi and Mia Verbeck. You both are the highlight of my life. I love you both dearly.

As always, thank you to my Lord and Savior for all He has taught me and for loving me enough to save me.

Introduction

It is hard to know where and how to set boundaries in relationships. It can feel like we master our boundaries in one area only to begin all over again in another. There are times we need to set and hold boundaries in the relationships we have, but there are definite barriers we face. We may feel guilty, be afraid to hurt someone's feelings, or be unsure of how to set and hold the boundary. Also, *when* are we supposed to set boundaries? What determines if we are supposed to set a boundary? If you are a Christian, for most of us, the larger goal is, "How do I set boundaries in a way that honors God?" The Faith Based Relationship Trust Boundary Model addresses each of these questions and concerns. The model will help you learn how to set boundaries regardless of the situation, under any circumstances, and in all types of relationships. You can learn this model once and use it for the rest of your life.

Before we can use this model, there a few things we need to understand. Number one is trust. What is trust and how do we use trust to help guide us in our relationships. Number 2 is boundaries. We have lots of boundaries, but for the sake of learning how to use the model, we just need to understand two of them. We will learn how to use the boundaries to protect our privacy. Number 3 is the different types of relationships we have and other contributing factors that complicate how boundaries are made and held in relationships. Lastly, we will discuss some verses from the bible to be sure we are aligning our boundary setting with the word of God. Please be sure you pray and read The Bible for yourself. Ask God if this is what He would have you do. I will share verses that stand out to me that support our need for boundaries.

Some of our most challenging boundary issues will come from our family, because some of our greatest disappointments and hurts stem from our family. For many Christians, it is familial relationships that cause us the most turmoil when it comes to setting boundaries in a way that aligns with scripture. We still hear the phrase "blood is thicker than water", which means… you do not ever betray your family because, "family is everything". A few years ago, I was speaking with my friend Nick McLaren and he reminded me of the quote, "The water of the womb is not thicker than the blood of the covenant." I had heard this quote before, but somehow, it was not sinking in enough to override the idea, "that family is everything". So, let's see if scripture supports this idea.

In Mark 3:31-35 (King James Version), Jesus defines who our brothers, sisters, and our mothers are.

[31] There came then his brethren and his mother, and, standing without, sent unto him, calling him.

[32] And the multitude sat about him, and they said unto him, Behold, thy mother and thy brethren without seek for thee.

[33] And he answered them, saying, Who is my mother, or my brethren?

[34] And he looked round about on them which sat about him, and said, Behold my mother and my brethren!

[35] For whosoever shall do the will of God, the same is my brother, and my sister, and mother.

Here we can see Jesus defining family as those who do the will of the father. This was done in comparison to his "water in womb" family. This moment supports the blood of the covenant as being thicker than the water of the womb.

In Matthew 10:34-37 (KJV), Jesus clearly defines what He has come to do, and He states that it is not to bring peace, but division to a home between those who believe and those who do not.

[34] Think not that I am come to send peace on earth: I came not to send peace, but a sword.

[35] For I am come to set a man at variance against his father, and the daughter against her mother, and the daughter in law against her mother in law.

³⁶ And a man's foes shall be they of his own household.

³⁷ He that loveth father or mother more than me is not worthy of me: and he that loveth son or daughter more than me is not worthy of me.

Here Jesus is telling us that our enemies can be in our own home when one believes and one does not. Jesus also goes on to say that if you love your mother, father, son, or daughter more than Him, you will not be worthy of Him. He is letting us know that He needs to be first above ALL, including family. We can see now from scripture that Nick was right, "the water of the womb is not thicker than the blood of the covenant".

If all of this sounds overwhelming, or way over your head, I can relate. As I write this it feels like "a lot!", but having boundaries is doable for anyone! This book will help you to break down the dynamics of boundaries in all of your relationships. By the time you are done reading it, you will be able to have more confidence in setting boundaries in relationships. The key, like anything, is do not give up and take one chapter at a time. My hope is for this book to bring you some knowledge and understanding so you can feel empowered in your relationships. Now let's dive in!

Chapter 1

Trust

Before we can dive into this idea of trust, we first need to understand our rights in relationships. When we have trauma or have experienced victimization, we can begin to believe we need others to give us our rights. This can cause us to try to demand that we be given rights, to fight for our rights, or to beg and plead for our rights. The truth is, we already possess our rights in relationships. What we want to learn to do instead, is to learn how to exercise our rights and not wait for someone to give us our rights or to respect our rights.

The model is going to teach us how to exercise our rights by learning what our right to privacy is. Once we have learned what our right to privacy is, we will learn how to protect our privacy through the use of boundaries. This is the purpose of the boundaries; we use the boundaries to protect our privacy and this is how we exercise our rights. Now let's look at this idea of trust.

If you want to be successful at having boundaries in relationships, you need to understand trust and what happens when trust is broken. You will learn how to use trust to help you to establish boundaries in a later chapter. For now, let's take a look at this idea of trust.

Somehow, when I was growing up, I got the message that I was supposed to trust everyone unless they "did me wrong", and if someone did me wrong, then it was my job to cut them out of my life. To be an untrusting person was taboo, it meant that you had issues and that you could not be trusted either. These rules set me up to trust the wrong people over and over. Not only that, but by the time I was "burned" by them, I had already established a bond with them and it seemed impossible to "cut" them out of my life. So not only was I trusting everyone, I was also bonding to people who were not good for me, and then I could not let them go. This made me feel weak and confused. This was my relationship with trust. Freely given and consistently broken to the point that I did not really even think about if I trusted someone or not. I did not have a gate that someone had to wait at to be let in, everyone got in all they had to do was try.

Trust is not something to just give away carelessly, it has to be earned. Although we would not want to trust someone that we do not know, we also do not trust someone just *because* we know them. We trust those that are trust worthy and we do not trust those that are untrustworthy. The question then becomes, "How do we know who is trustworthy and who is not?" Trust takes time, because it is built over time in a relationship. The following is a list of characteristics that you may find in a trustworthy person:

1. They are loyal and reliable

2. Their words align with their actions

3. You do not catch them lying to other people

4. They do not talk bad about other people behind their back and then pretend to be their best friend

5. They do not steal

6. They show empathy

7. They feel guilt when they wrong someone

8. They respect your boundaries

Once you have decided to trust someone and you have allowed them to get close to you, things can change and that trust can be broken. When trust is broken, we tend to have a sudden decrease in trust with that person. Once apologies have been made and a reconciliation occurs, the expectation is that trust goes right back to the same level it was at prior to being broken. This, often times, becomes a barrier to healing. We are expected to trust and to be vulnerable with someone that just broke our trust. Trusting someone that we now see as untrustworthy is not natural for us, even if we really want to trust that person again. Everything in us, is telling us to "watch out!", "be careful" and to not get too close to this person. We may feel pressure to act as if things are right back to normal or to act as though we do trust this person again. Part of us may just be tired of hurting. The pressure can also come from wanting to feel close to this person again and enjoy the freedom that came from trust. It can also be pressure from the person that broke the trust.

It is important to take a moment to speak to how difficult it can be to express your need for more time. Broken trust is often painful for both the person that broke the trust as well as the one who's trust was broken. I have heard things like, "You don't love me, if you cannot trust me, what is the point", "I already said I was sorry, how long are you going to hold on to this", "You should trust me, I love you", all in response to someone still struggling to trust after trust was broken. If someone broke your trust, and is now demanding that you trust them again, they may not realize that broken trust takes time to rebuild. It is not based off of how much you love them, want to be with them, or want to trust them again, it is simply based off of time and evidence of trustworthy actions. If the person continues with the behavior that broke your trust, you will more than likely not be able to rebuild trust with them.

Trust takes time, so if you were lied to, cheated on or betrayed in some other manner, please know that someone guilting you, threatening you or pressuring you to trust them again, is not ok, it is not healthy. Now that you know and are beginning to understand that building trust takes time, hopefully you give yourself permission to need the time it takes for you to rebuild trust. I would encourage you to express that need and to not buy into the pressure. You do not have to trust overnight, in fact you more than likely will not. You cannot make yourself trust someone, when you do not trust them. It is something that has to be built over time and if you are dealing with an untrustworthy person, you may never be able to build that trust, because you are not supposed to. We do not want to teach ourselves to ignore our gut and trust someone that is not trustworthy.

It is helpful to realize that trust does not equal forgiveness. You can forgive someone, and know that you cannot trust them. Learning that trust takes time to build and rebuild, gives you permission to just be where you are at with that person. You do not have to reconcile or trust right away. You get to say, "I am sorry, I still do not trust you. I think I will need more time to know that I can trust you again." We can forgive, but that does not equal trust, and we do not fully reconcile until trust is rebuilt. It can be helpful to learn to separate the ideas of trust, forgiveness, and reconciliation.

Next, let's take a look at what the Bible has to say about manipulation, deceit, and trust. In Romans 16:17-18 (KJV) we learn there will be some we will need to turn away from. The Apostle Paul also gives us insight on how we are deceived.

[17] Now I beseech you, brethren, mark them which cause divisions and offences contrary to the doctrine which ye have learned; and avoid them.

[18] For they that are such serve not our Lord Jesus Christ, but their own belly; and by good words and fair speeches deceive the hearts of the simple.

The Apostle Paul is telling us that we will be deceived by words. We need to limit the amount of time we give our ears to someone if they have proven to be untrustworthy. Those that have earned our trust, get to be closer to our ears. Here is another example of where we are warned about the danger of allowing someone who is untrustworthy to give us their words. Judges 16:16 (KJV)

[16] And it came to pass, when she pressed him daily with her words, and urged him, so that his soul was vexed unto death;

This verse is talking about Delilah. Delilah was a woman who was hired by Samson's enemies to discover Samson's weakness for the purposes of overtaking him. Samson was in love with Delilah, but to Delilah, Samson was a job. Delilah was not as strong as Samson physically, but she used something more powerful than his strength, her words. We will discuss their story more in a later chapter. This a very sad example of what can happen to us when we do not move away from someone who is not trustworthy for us, whether we love them or not.

Psalm 118:8-9 (KJV) tells where to put our greatest trust.

[8] It is better to trust in the LORD than to put confidence in man.
[9] It is better to trust in the LORD than to put confidence in princes.

Here we learn, that above every type of relationship you have, the Lord is the **best** place to put your trust. We give the most trust to the Lord. It can be hard to tell if you are giving the most trust to the Lord, but The Faith Based Relationship Trust Boundary Model is going to help you define how to do that as well.

To summarize, we do not want to trust everyone right off of the bat. Trust takes time to build, broken trust takes time to rebuild, and we give the Lord more trust than all of our other relationships. We can learn traits of trustworthy people as well as traits of untrustworthy people to help us better decide who we are going to trust and who we need to be more cautious around and possibly not trust, maybe ever. We will circle back to the idea of trust and to use our level of trust to help us with the boundaries we need in our relationships.

Chapter 2

Boundaries-Emotional and Physical

Next, we will look at the idea of boundaries. Boundaries help us to feel safe and to feel close to others. Understanding boundaries and learning how to hold boundaries empowers us in our relationships. For most of us, our first lessons in boundaries came in childhood. What we were taught about boundaries shapes how we hold boundaries with others in adulthood, or not hold boundaries in adulthood.

There are several areas that boundaries exist in. For the sake of the model, we will look at two areas of boundaries: physical and emotional. These two areas will help to us to establish how close we will allow someone to get to us both physically and emotionally. Let's start by looking at the physical boundaries.

We will define physical boundaries by how proximally close you are to someone or by proximity. For example, right now my dog is about 2 feet away from me and my TV is about 6 feet away from me, this would result in my dog being proximally closer to me than my television. When we are discussing where we want/need to place the people in our lives with physical boundaries, we can measure that in terms of distance, how physically close or far from us they are. This also includes things like touching. If someone is touching us, then we have fewer physical boundaries with them than someone who is not allowed to touch us. Often times, the relationship type is going to determine the physical boundary.

Switching over to emotional boundaries now, we will define those as the extent to which we emote with someone. How much of ourselves emotionally we give to someone or let them emote with us, determines our emotional boundaries. When looking at emotional boundaries we will see that there are things we share and things that we keep private. If you share everything, then you have no privacy, hence you have no emotional boundaries. For the sake of the model, we will define emotional boundaries based on how much you share of what is in your head, and what is in your heart.

Here is a list of some examples of what is in our heads and hearts:

1. Our thoughts

2. Our feelings

3. Our fears

4. Our worries

5. Our dreams

6. Our past failures

7. Our past traumas

8. Our disappointments

In other words, how much you share of what is in your head, and heart, is the extent to which you are emoting with someone. If you are telling someone lots of what is in your head and in your heart, you are emoting to a great extent with them which means you are having fewer emotional boundaries. If you give someone very little of what is in your head and in your heart, you are emoting very little with them and you are having stronger emotional boundaries.

SELF

Moving forward, when we use the model, you will notice the bottom heart has the word self in the middle. When we talk about "self" in the model, this includes everything that is in your head, your heart, and your physical body. This is All yours and this is all **private**. You get to decide what you want to share with others in these areas. When referring to your right to privacy, that is acknowledging your right to decide how much you want to share in each of these areas.

If we are following the advice from Psalms 118:8-9 and putting our greatest trust in the Lord, our relationship with the Lord would need to look different than every other relationship we have. This means, we give most of our trust to Him. We share most of "self" with Him, so He gets full access to everything in our head and everything in our heart. When we give the most trust to Him, we get closer to Him than anyone else in our lives. This is where our strength comes from, this is how we build a relationship with Him. When we are closest to Him and we go through something hard, we are not easily broken. However, if we give more trust to any other relationship we have, and we go through something hard, it can break us. Moving forward, we want to be sure we are giving most of **self** to the Lord, this is us putting our greatest trust in the One who gave it all.

To summarize, anything in your head (thoughts, fears, worries) or in your heart (hopes, hurts, disappointments), and your physical body all belongs to *self* and that is where the boundaries start for your sense of privacy. This space is reserved for you and the Lord alone. No one goes in self except and the Lord. This is also what is your right to protect. When you are protecting your right to privacy, you are exercising your right to decide how much of "self" you wish to share with another. We learn from Proverbs 13:3 (KJV)

[3] He that keepeth his mouth keepeth his life: but he that openeth wide his lips shall have destruction.

Moving forward, when we are trying to establish boundaries, we need to look at both of these areas to see where we need to set and hold a boundary. How physically close we allow someone to be to us and how much we emote (to what extent we share our thoughts, feelings dreams, etc.) makes up our emotional and physical boundaries, and we alone get to decide that. The physical boundary is often defined by the relationship type and the emotional boundary is based on how much trust has been earned and your role in the relationship. If reading this is overwhelming, take a break and come back to it when you are ready. It will become clearer when we discuss the model.

Chapter 3

Relationships

Next, let's look at another area we will be using to establish boundaries; relationships. We have relationships with our family members, co-workers, acquaintances, partner, strangers, friends, best-friend, classmates, etc. Some of our relational interactions occur daily, while other interactions or encounters will be less often. When we look at these different relationships we have in our lives, we would want to be able to differentiate those that we are close to vs. those that we are less close with.

For example, we are more than likely closer to our best-friend than we are to a stranger. This may seem silly to point out, but it may surprise some of us, when we look at the boundaries we are having with both groups. Some of us may share just as much with a stranger as we would our best friend. This would be an issue with boundaries in relationships and it is rooted in trust. We are trusting a complete stranger as much as we are trusting our best-friend, this is unwise and it will cause us to feel small, young or helpless when in fact we are not.

One exercise that is helpful at this point is to write down a list of the categories of relationships you have in your life. Some examples may include: strangers, friends, family, partner, etc. Once you have written the categories down, re-write them in order starting with the level you share *you* most with and continue on down to the level that you share the least with. If you have categories that you share with at an equal level just write both groups on the same line. Once you have written your categories down, look at your list and see if it makes sense. Is the level that you are sharing your private self with, where you want it to be or do you want to make some changes? Can you see any issues with how you are sharing?

Now that you have your categories labeled, let's decide the extent of self that you would want to share in the different categories. If partner is closest to self, then no one would get more than your partner. Your partner gets the most of your hopes, dreams, fears, disappointments etc. The same is true with the physical boundaries, no one has more physical access to you than partner. When we share more with a friend or co-worker than we do with our partner, this is how emotional affairs occur. When a coworker has the same physical boundaries as a partner, this is also how a physical affair occurs.

If we catch ourselves sharing self on the same level as partner with someone that is not our partner, we need to address this by putting an emotional or physical boundary in place and not share to this extent with this person. The same is true with a potential partner who is not a committed partner yet. This person would not go in partner level because they have not earned that level of trust yet. This level of trust is earned over time and involves **commitment**. Many individuals that are new to dating tend to make that mistake because the "new" person has the potential to be a "partner" they have less privacy with them right out of the gate. Instead of starting them at stranger level and then allowing trust to grow and working towards their place as partner, they go straight into partner level with little to no boundaries or privacy.

Below is a chart of what we might share based on the type of relationship we have with that person.

Stranger
- Surface level - weather, things you may see or hear in that moment
- Polite
- Nothing Personal
- Brief Interactions

Acquaintance
- Nothing deep-surface level thoughts
- Can share some interests (surface level)
- No past issues or tramas are shared

Coworker
- Can share some interests
- Can share more on thoughts and hopes -work related
- Over time, once trust is built you can share more personal information but not on a friend level if they are still at coworker level

Friend
- Share more private things with friends
- Hopes, fears, thoughts
- Will share at different levels with different friends

Family
- Share at different levels with different family members
- Do not have to share anything you are not comfortable with
- Your business is not automatically your familie's business
- You have a right to privacy

Partner
- Gets most of "self" both physical and emotional
- If you have a partner it's important that only partner goes here
- Sharing at this level with children parentifies them
- Holding emotional and physical boundaries at this level protects the partnership, do this by only sharing at this level with your partner
- If you do not have a partner, share your emotional self through journaling

Self
- This level is reserved for your most private self
- Greatest dreams and fears
- Past traumas and shameful experiences, most private thoughts and feelings
- You protect yourself by holding emotional boundaries and controlling which parts of self you decide to share,
- You still have a right to privacy even with a partner

When someone is single and feeling lonely, or in a relationship and feeling lonely, chances are it is because they don't feel like they have someone in that partner level that they can share self to that degree with. This is why we feel lonely. If we are single, we can either try to find a person that we can build trust with over time until they are in that level, or share different parts of ourselves with friends and family until we have a partner to feel that level. Until then, we can share self by journaling, meditating on His word, or any other form that allows you to acknowledge and connect with self. Share what is in your head and in your heart with the Lord. Tell Him what you are thinking and feeling. Feeling lonely when you're not sharing self at a partner level is normal, and it is okay. You can use this time to strengthen your relationship with yourself and with the Lord and then find yourself feeling less lonely. Next, let's take a look at roles and how they can help us to keep our sharing appropriate.

ROLES

When deciding what is safe and healthy to share, we also want to factor in **roles**. What is our role/responsibility in the relationship. For example, let us say I am going to share with a family member. In this case the family member is my child. My role in the relationship is parent. I would want to factor my role in the relationship before I share. I would not share to the same extent with my child as I would with an adult family member that I trust. Considering our role in the relationship helps us to keep our sharing safe, healthy, and appropriate.

What is Expected of Us?

Before we jump into the model and how it works, let's first take a look at some scriptures that outline what is expected of us as believers and followers of Christ in our relationships. Romans 12:18 (KJV) teaches us our responsibility in how to live with others.

18 If it is possible, as far as it depends on you, live at peace with everyone.

Paul is telling us to live at peace with everyone. We are not to be critical of others, cause rifts with fighting and arguing, or any other way we may be tempted to disrupt the peace. As we will see from other scriptures that does not mean be a doormat or have no boundaries. If we can turn the other cheek and choose not to say the cutting words we sometimes want to, we are more likely to be living in peace with others. So does this mean we are supposed to be around anyone who wants to be around us? Check out 1 Corinthians 15:33 (KJV),

33 Be not deceived: evil communications corrupt good manners.

When we allow someone who is deceptive or who is bad company to get close to us and have access to our ears, we change and usually not for the better. We are not supposed to be close to those that are deceptive. This is someone who is manipulative, lies, or has bad intentions for us. So why is it so important that we have good morals?

Let's see what Jesus has to say about this in Matthew 5:13-16 (KJV);

[13] Ye are the salt of the earth: but if the salt have lost his savour, wherewith shall it be salted? it is thenceforth good for nothing, but to be cast out, and to be trodden under foot of men.

[14] Ye are the light of the world. A city that is set on an hill cannot be hid.

[15] Neither do men light a candle, and put it under a bushel, but on a candlestick; and it giveth light unto all that are in the house.

[16] Let your light so shine before men, that they may see your good works, and glorify your Father which is in heaven.

If bad company corrupts us, we will become watered down and lose our saltiness. If we are to be the light of the world, we need to be sure we are not allowing ourselves be corrupted. The model is going to help us to learn how to do this while doing our part to maintain peace.

Matthew 5:37 (KJV), Jesus helps us to not be manipulative and also helps us to watch out for manipulative speech.

[37] But let your communication be, Yea, yea; Nay, nay: for whatsoever is more than these cometh of evil.

It is not our job to talk someone into something. When we say no or yes it needs to mean exactly that. If you catch yourself trying to talk someone into something, you may be getting manipulative. Likewise, if you have already given your yes or your no and someone continues to try to get an answer from you, you may be being manipulated. This is another thing that is expected of us, to be clear and mean what we say and to be mindful that anything more than this comes from the evil one.

We are called to forgive this is clearly seen in scripture. In Luke 17:3-4 (KJV) Jesus states,

[3] Take heed to yourselves: If thy brother trespass against thee, rebuke him; and if he repent, forgive him.

[4] And if he trespass against thee seven times in a day, and seven times in a day turn again to thee, saying, I repent; thou shalt forgive him.

So, does this mean we are just supposed to be reconciling with someone over and over again? Let's look at what Jesus has to say about what to do when someone wrongs you. In Matthew 18:15-17 (KJV) He states;

[15] Moreover if thy brother shall trespass against thee, go and tell him his fault between thee and him alone: if he shall hear thee, thou hast gained thy brother.

¹⁶ But if he will not hear thee, then take with thee one or two more, that in the mouth of two or three witnesses every word may be established.

¹⁷ And if he shall neglect to hear them, tell it unto the church: but if he neglect to hear the church, let him be unto thee as an heathen man and a publican.

This passage points to our role when someone has wronged us. We are to go directly to that person first to discuss the issue. When we struggle with codependency, we tend to go to everyone except the person the issue is with. Learning how to confront and resolve conflict is a must if we struggle with this. Verse 17 shows me that we are to treat those who are unwilling to hear, acknowledge, and deal with the issue as strangers. We are no longer required to be close to them. Proverbs 4:23-27 (KJV) share a similar message:

²³ Keep thy heart with all diligence; for out of it are the issues of life.

²⁴ Put away from thee a froward mouth, and perverse lips put far from thee.

²⁵ Let thine eyes look right on, and let thine eyelids look straight before thee.

²⁶ Ponder the path of thy feet, and let all thy ways be established.

²⁷ Turn not to the right hand nor to the left: remove thy foot from evil.

Isn't it interesting that part of guarding our heart involves not allowing perverse lips near us. This can apply both to our own as well as to others. We will clearly see the consequence of not doing so in the story of Samson and Delilah.

Next, we will use the model to see how we pull all of this information together and use it to help us to establish boundaries in relationships based on trust. Once we know the level that individuals fall in, based off of trust and our role in the relationship, it becomes clearer how to establish and hold boundaries with the people in our lives. We will hold boundaries by how much of self we give, both physically and emotionally.

Chapter 4

The Relationship Trust Boundary Model

Now that we have done the hard work of understanding trust, relationships and boundaries, we are ready to see how this model works. The key to using this model, is to allow trust and your role in the relationship to establish where you are going to place someone within the model. Trust and our role are the gauge for where someone goes, and then we establish and hold the boundaries using physical and emotional boundaries to keep us safe and whole. You always emote out from self. You start at self and decide what you are going to share in your relationships. No one goes in self but you and the Lord. You protect your right to privacy and hold your boundaries by not allowing anyone to go in **self** except you and the Lord.

Remember, the closer someone is to self the more we emote with them. The further someone is placed from self the less we share with them, or the more privacy we keep. This is also true for physical boundaries. The further someone is from self, the less physical contact they have with us, and the closer someone is to self the more physical contact they will have with us. Below is a diagram of an example of what healthy level relationship placement may look like. You may choose to change some of the categories within the different levels. For some of us, we are closer to our best-friend than we are to our family, in that case, you would place best-friend closer to self than family.

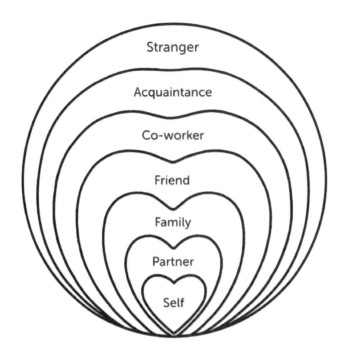

Next, make your own bullseye like chart for your relationship categories in relation to self if you have different categories of people in your life. Feel free to move the categories around and add or take any away that you need or do not need. The one recommendation is to always keep the stranger, acquaintance, partner, and the self-categories as they are. This is important because it will give you a reference for sharing. However, feel free to change any of the categories in between these four to better represent the relationships you have in your life. After you place the relationships in the different levels on the bullseye, think about what it means in terms of what you will share in each level based on how much you trust them and your role. It is possible for the people in our lives to move closer to self, this occurs because over time you may begin to build trust with that person, so they get more of self. For example, let's say you begin to know a coworker over time, they are showing who they are in terms of their character. You decide that this is a person you would like to get to know more, so you start to go to lunch or out of coffee. As you get to know them more and if you trust them more, they can move into the friend level if you decide they have earned enough trust from you to do so.

The opposite is also true, individuals can move further out from self when they break your trust. For example, if you catch someone lying to you or cheating on you or betraying your trust in some way, you can move them into a level that is further from self. Even though they are not a stranger, you can place them in the stranger level and only share self with them to the extent you would a stranger. Once and if trust is re-established, they can move through the levels and they can become closer to self again in time, and it will take time.

Couples I have seen that have broken trust want to mend quickly and force the trust. This causes damage and prolongs healing, oftentimes it guarantees the end of the relationship. If someone cheats, and the couple reconciles, then they want trust to be immediate. They may say things like, "It's never going to work if you don't trust me", or "I thought you forgave me, but clearly you haven't", or "If you don't trust me, there's no point, this won't work". In reality, if time and space is not given to the person whose trust was broken, there can be no trust rebuilt.

The following diagram is an example of how you may place your partner in a different level for a period of time until trust is rebuilt.

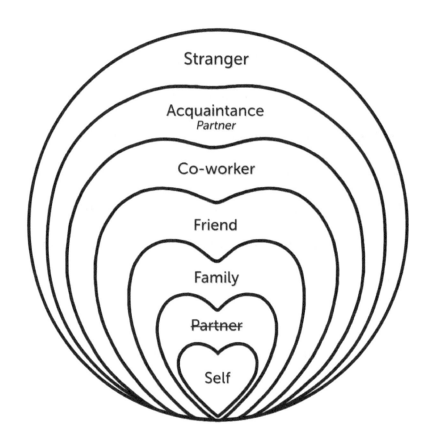

If trust is rebuilt, your partner can slowly begin to work into the next level all the way until they are back in the space where partner is supposed to go. While you are healing, it may help to journal or see a therapist so you can share private thoughts and emotions. Journaling our thoughts and emotions helps us not to feel so alone to the point where it is clouding our judgement. Remember, taking your hurt the mighty Counselor is the best plan. He does not promise to fix every part of your life the way you want Him to, but He will transform you by renewing your mind.

Using this model will also help you deal with difficult family members or people that you have to be around that you do not trust. For example, let's say I have a sister that I just found out betrayed me, and now it is Thanksgiving dinner and I have to go be near her. She is technically in the family level, but I may trust her at the same level I trust an acquaintance. Due to the fact that she is family, I may not be able to physically keep her at the same distance as an acquaintance, but I can hold my emotional boundary by protecting my privacy and only sharing self at the same level I would share with someone who was an acquaintance. Here is an example of what this might look like.

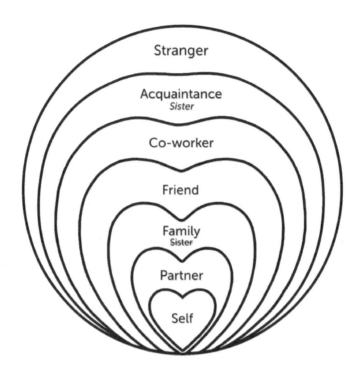

The level I share at would be surface level, I would keep it cordial but I would stay away from things that are deeper or more private to me, some examples I may not be discussing are: children, personal issues, worries etc. This is one way I can go to Thanksgiving and not feel small, or like I do not have any rights and I have to be someone's best-friend that I know is just using me. I also would not be as physically close to her as I would be to other family members. It would not be my priority to spend the most time with her, I would spend time with her like I might with an acquaintance. This is how I can set and hold boundaries until trust is rebuilt.

Boundary Issues Explained by the Model

Here are some examples of boundary issues explained using the model.

Codependency:

When any us of struggles with codependency, we are trying to relate and connect by going into someone's "self". We want full access to everything about them. We may even try to control the way they think, feel and act. This can be anything from controlling what they eat for lunch to demanding to know what they are thinking and feeling. Remember, no one goes in self but you and the Lord and you emote out from there. Also, we need to stay in the partner level and not try to push to be in the self-level of our partner's model. This allows them to share in a way that helps them to feel safe.

Parentification:

This can occur when we have a child that we are emoting with at the partner level. Having a child be placed in this level causes us to abandon the emotional needs of the child. Now they are listening to us emote and they may begin to believe they are responsible for more than they are capable of handling. This can lead to all sorts of issues we do not want for our children. This is one example of how remembering our role in the relationship helps us to keep our sharing appropriate.

Church Hurt:

When we enter into a church, most of us are allowing strangers to immediately go into the family level. We are vulnerable and do not have many emotional boundaries in place. This is because we enter with high levels of trust. In truth, these strangers may become our family, but for now they are strangers. Being this vulnerable before trust is built can help to explain why when we experience a hurt at church it cuts deep.

Professionals:

If we are a professional, we will serve a population or group of people that will more than likely share a great deal with us. It can feel unnatural or rude to not share at the same level as someone else. In addition to the level they share with us, we may work with some individuals for an extended period time.

Over time, we can feel trust being built in the working relationship and may be tempted to allow them to get closer to "self" in our model. This again is where we need to be mindful of our role in the relationship. Although we can be very close to their "self" in their model, based off our role they need be further from "self "in our model.

This is where it can be helpful to add a level in your model. For example, if I am a teacher, I may add a level for students and write what is appropriate to share at this new level. This level for students would more than likely be closer to coworker or acquaintance. Each of us has our own model. Although someone may be giving us more trust because of our role in their life, it does not mean we automatically match them with our level of trust in our model. Remember our role in the relationship will help to guide us in where we place individuals within our model.

There is no limit to the number of levels you can add. Feel free to add in as many as you need to be clear on the boundaries you have. Any time there is a relationship you have that is not on the model, decide which level you feel safe sharing at, then add the category. If you want, you can also combine more than one type of relationship in a particular level.

For example, let's say you have a coparenting relationship. You will need to first decide how much trust is in the relationship, then add a category for that relationship in the model. Let's say you trust the person you are coparenting with at a coworker level, you can add a / in the coworker level and write **coparent**. This would mean you feel safe sharing about the child and how **you feel** about the child. However, if there is less trust with the other parent, you may want to add coparent to acquaintance. This would mean you share about the child, but not necessarily how you feel about the child. If the other coparent and you have lots of trust they could go in family or friend.

When organizing the model so it works for you, remember, I would recommend you keep self, partner, acquaintance, and stranger where they are. This helps to give you a healthy point of reference when you are deciding what is safe and appropriate to share for the different types of relationships you have. Then you can make a list of what is on the table and what is off the table in terms of sharing so you are clear where the boundaries are.

Chapter 5

Privacy and Trauma's Impact on Privacy

If you grew up in a home where you were not allowed to have boundaries, physical or emotional, then you did not have any privacy or maybe you had little privacy. When we are not given our right to privacy, we do not learn the concept of self and we do not learn to share in a safe way. This happens because we do not understand our right to privacy. People in our lives are either in or out, we either share nothing or everything. It is empowering when we realize that we do not have to answer someone's question. When you grow up with trauma or in a home that has no boundaries (does not allow for privacy), then you feel pressure to give anyone full access to self, even strangers.

So, how does this happen in homes? Here is a list of bullet points that illustrate some examples of how lines between boundaries, trust and relationships get blurred.

- If you were hit (Someone violated your physical boundary)
- If you were sexually abused (Someone violated your physical and emotional boundary, remember that space is reserved for partner only. If someone forced themselves in that space then it can be less clear later on how someone earns the right to that space through trust. Having our private selves exposed to another in a way that

we did not give consent, or having someone expose their private selves to us in a way that we did not give consent, makes the line for boundaries blurry)

- If you were forced to expose private areas of your body (You may feel less protective over your body because someone else was in charge of it)

- If you were not allowed to shut your bedroom door (You may feel like everyone has right to see and know what you are doing at all times, and they do not. You have a right to privacy; you choose what you share)

- If someone in the home had the right to read your diary or journal (You may not have learned up to this point in our life, you get to find a space that is just yours where you can exist and get to know yourself more, and this place is yours alone to protect and guard)

- If you were not allowed to have private conversations (You may feel pressure to share everything you talk about with one person to another person. Often times you feel you have to share all of your conversations with your partner or others. You do not, you are allowed to have privacy, if you are having conversations that would break trust between you and your partner, then that is something different. Overall, you are allowed privacy and so is your partner)

- If you were taught not telling someone everything is the same as lying (This is not the same as lying, you are allowed privacy, you have a right to privacy. You get to decide what you do and do not share; it is not lying and it is not rude. It is rude if someone asks something that is none of their business, it is not rude to not share, that is your right)

We heal through sharing. When we share our shame and our toxic shame we begin to heal, but we need to be sharing with those that have earned our trust and have shown to be a trustworthy person. When we have trauma, we try to share with anyone that will listen or we never share and the shame and toxic shame comes out in other ways like substance abuse, anger management issues, isolation or withdrawing. This does not help us to heal, in fact, often times it leads to further trauma. When we are sharing our scariest parts of self with someone before they have earned our trust, it re-violates us and the shame deepens, especially if they are not a trustworthy person.

Abuse, can lay a foundation for misunderstanding what it means to be physically close to someone. This is how we can sit next to a stranger on a bus and feel like we have to share everything with them or want to share everything with them. No boundaries, no rights to privacy, this the byproduct of abuse. This stranger gets access to **self**, without ever having to earn your trust. *We need to learn that physical closeness does not equal emotional closeness and it certainly does not equal trust*. You will have moments in your life where you will be physically close to a stranger (like sitting next to someone on a bus). You hold your boundaries and protect self by not giving up your privacy. Meaning you do not share very much of self with a stranger.

There are other trust issues worth mentioning. If you have a difficult time allowing your partner to have access to more parts of self than a coworker, then you will have issues in your relationship. Let us say, for example, you have been with your partner for a period of time and they have never given you a reason not to trust them and although you may be physical with them, you emote or share self at the same level you would with a co-worker. Your partner is going to feel this just as you may feel this from a partner. If you or your partner is not emoting at a partner level, doing some sharing exercises can help to strengthen the trust as well as teach you both how to share with each other. These exercises can include taking turns asking questions. Here are a few questions you can use as examples:

- What are you most worried about right now?

- What are you afraid of?

- What makes you happy?

- What is your fondest childhood memory?

- What has been your greatest disappointment?

Asking and answering these personal and private questions over time, helps to get and to feel closer. However, this is not something that can be forced, it would need to be both parties agreeing to engage in an effort to get closer.

Understanding the level of trust we are placing in someone when we give them access to self, explains why those that hold a professional license are held to higher consequence when they break that trust. When you visit a professional like a Dr., or a therapist, the societal expectation is that you share pieces of yourself physically and or emotionally that are private with a stranger. You are putting a great deal of trust in them because of the professional license they hold and you are letting down your boundaries, making you very vulnerable. It is this level of vulnerability that the law and regulations protect because you have a right to privacy.

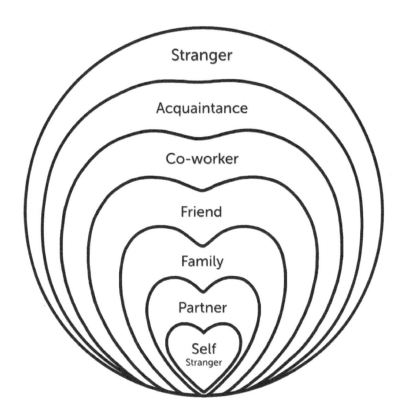

As we learn more and more about predators, we are beginning to see that we still need and have the right to privacy, even if we are seeing a professional. If your gut says something is off, you do not have to share part of self with that person, regardless of the license they carry. We still need to have some boundaries up and allow trust to be built over time. We have the right to our privacy and we get to protect **self** no matter who it is or the situation we are in. We get to say, "I am not comfortable answering that right now, or, "I am not ready for that type of an examination right now, I will get back to you when and if I decide to go ahead with that." Once we understand our right to privacy, things begin to change for us, especially in the boundaries we have in relationships and what we share.

Chapter 6

Moving forward

At this point, you may be beating yourself up or thinking of all the times that you have had poor boundaries and either embarrassed yourself or struggled in relationships because of poor boundaries. Maybe you trusted someone when they gave you no reason too and you shared too much. Maybe for not being able to stick up for yourself and say, "Yeah, I am not answering that, it's inappropriate for you to ask". Or, you are being hard on yourself for not knowing how to deal with your personal relationships when trust has been broken. This is normal, I did the same thing.

Hopefully there comes a point for all of us where we stop beating ourselves up and decide to move forward. No more poor boundaries, no more feeling used, disappointed in relationships, or helpless. We can make the decision to grow, to get better at holding the boundaries and protecting ourselves. I like to think about the way a plant grows. It always reaches for the sun. If you place your plant facing north and the sun is coming from the east, it will grow reaching for the east. If you then turn that plant a different direction, rather than the plant beating itself up, it just begins to lean the other way. It will always grow and reach towards the light.

Remember, we share more of ourselves with those that earn our trust. We do not have to answer a question simply because it is asked or let someone in our emotional boundaries just because they pry. Trust is earned over time and if it is broken, then we have the right to emotionally and physically distance ourselves from the person that broke our trust.

This model can work for you, and it will help you to protect yourself and to heal. I encourage you to make this book and model your own. You decide what you will share in each level based off how much trust you are giving to someone as well as deciding which relationships you place in the levels. Again, I recommend self, partner and stranger do not move when you create your model. The relationships you struggle with most, would be a great place to start. Draw your model and write people's names in the different categories based on the level of trust you have with them and your role in the relationship. This will give you an idea of how much you will share parts of self with.

Here is an example:

Below is a list of Becky's relationships. She has placed them in her diagram based on the level of trust she has for them along with her role in the relationship. The physical boundary is based on relationship type and the emotional boundary is based on the role and level of trust. We write individuals in our diagram based on the emotional boundary.

Ralph- Brother that I trust

Sarah- Sister that broke trust and is working towards rebuilding trust

Mike- Boss that I am not sure I trust yet

Jake- Partner that I trust

Sue- friend that I trust

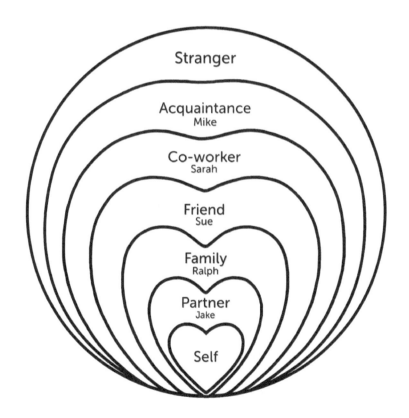

Now that the relationships have been placed in the model based off of the level of trust and her role in each of them, Becky has a better idea of how much of self she gives to each of these people until more trust is earned. This way Becky can be around them and not feel exposed or vulnerable. She can feel empowered to hold boundaries and not to over share. This also addresses people pleasing behaviors and retraumatizing ourselves.

Once you have completed your model by placing the people in your life in their appropriate levels, based on how much you trust them and your role in the relationship, place the model where you can see it. Reviewing the model before you go around the person you are struggling to hold boundaries with helps you to remember not share so much of self. When you backslide and catch yourself sharing too much of self, look at it. What prompted you to over share? Was it the amount of time spent with that person or was it because they asked very personal questions? Did they open up and share personal information first? Remember, you have a right to privacy and if you are sharing very personal information with a stranger, it is more than likely not a cosmic meeting. That individual can be a narcissist, maybe it's two people trauma bonding, or some other unhealthy issue. Just because someone shares, does not mean you have to share, and just because someone asks does not mean you have to answer.

Now as promised let's look at one example of someone who did not follow the model, Samson. We start off learning how vulnerable Samson was when he entered this relationship. Judges 16:4 (KJV) tells us he loved a woman whose name was Delilah. Samson was in love with Delilah, but for Delilah, Samson was a job. Delilah was paid to find Samson's weakness so he could be overtaken. Already we are seeing that our **love** for someone is **not** a reason to give them our full trust. Remember, we trust those who are trustworthy. Delilah had evil intentions for Samson, but because he loved her, he allowed her and her deceiving lips to get close to him and it cost him everything.

In this next portion, we see how Delilah uses her words to ensure Samson's demise. Judges 16:15-22 (KJV): (bold portions added)

[15] And she said unto him, **How canst thou say, I love thee**, when thine heart is not with me? thou hast mocked me these three times, and hast not told me wherein thy great strength lieth.

[16] And it came to pass, when she pressed him daily with her words, and urged him, so that his soul was vexed unto death;

¹⁷ That he told her all his heart, and said unto her, There hath not come a razor upon mine head; for I have been a Nazarite unto God from my mother's womb: if I be shaven, then my strength will go from me, and I shall become weak, and be like any other man.

¹⁸ And when Delilah saw that he had told her all his heart, she sent and called for the lords of the Philistines, saying, Come up this once, for he hath shewed me all his heart. Then the lords of the Philistines came up unto her, and brought money in their hand.

¹⁹ And she made him sleep upon her knees; and she called for a man, and she caused him to shave off the seven locks of his head; and she began to afflict him, and his strength went from him.

²⁰ And she said, The Philistines be upon thee, Samson. And he awoke out of his sleep, and said, I will go out as at other times before, and shake myself. And he wist not that the LORD was departed from him.

²¹ But the Philistines took him, and put out his eyes, and brought him down to Gaza, and bound him with fetters of brass; and he did grind in the prison house.

I hope you are catching how manipulative she was. She starts off by assigning Samson the task to prove to her he loves her, and she is letting him know he can prove his love by what? By allowing her full access to **self.** She wants what is most private. She wants access to information that was shared between Samson and the Lord. Remember, we must have a portion of our lives that is reserved for God alone. Prior to this Moment, she had already been showing Samson that he could not trust her. However, Samson did not make any changes in the relationship. Proverbs 5:3-5 (KJV)

³ For the lips of a strange woman drop as an honeycomb, and her mouth is smoother than oil:

⁴ But her end is bitter as wormwood, sharp as a two-edged sword.

⁵ Her feet go down to death; her steps take hold on hell.

When someone shows us we cannot trust them, we need to create distance emotionally and sometimes physically. We create emotional distance by giving them less of what is in our head and hearts. However, Samson did what most of us do. We keep talking and allowing them access to our ears. Going back to Proverbs 13:3 (KJV), when we guard our lips, we protect our lives.

³ He that keepeth his mouth keepeth his life: but he that openeth wide his lips shall have destruction.

After reading the story of Samson and Delilah we see the reality of Proverbs 5 and 13. These age-old principles apply to us **today**. When someone betrays us and we see the deceit and the bad intentions they have for us, we need to make a change in the relationship. We need to confront the issue and go to them directly. If they will not resolve it, will not talk about it, will not acknowledge it, we place them in stranger. If they never work towards addressing the issue or earning back our trust, they stay there. It does not matter who it is. It does not matter how much we love them. Samson loved

Delilah. She showed him he could not trust her; yet he stayed just as close to her physically and emotionally after each betrayal. In the end, he broke his Nazarite vow he had with God, had his eyes gouged out, and landed in prison.

It is not much different for us. When we keep someone close to us that we cannot trust, eventually we are pulled from our walk with God, we no longer see clearly, and become imprisoned. When someone betrays you, it is your job, your right, and your responsibility to put some distance between them and yourself. We do this by giving them less emotionally, thereby protecting our privacy. We guard what is in our head and what is in our heart. We do this by NOT TELLING THEM anything that is private. Delilah wanted access to all that was private. She was only satisfied and left Samson alone when she realized he had told her everything that was in his head and everything that was in his heart. Remember we guard our hearts and our lives when we close our mouths and keep deceitful people away from our ears.

My hope is for this book and model to empower you to take your life back and learn how to guard your heart. Trust in the Lord and rely on the Holy Spirit **most**. Make this your closest relationship. How ever you learned unhealthy trust, or poor boundaries in relationships, be the plant and lean a new way. Protect yourself and feel great about it, this is what we are supposed to do! Take good care, and thank you for spending this time with me to learn how to guard your heart so you can live in the freedom that has been bought for you. Remember to give Him more trust than anyone else in your life. The Son is there for you my friend…reach for Him and live in peace!

Reference:

King James Bible: Public Domain

Made in United States
Troutdale, OR
08/16/2024

22054925R00040